Cooking

Real Meals

in a

Hotel

Room

About the Author

Laura Sommers is **The Recipe Lady!**

She is the #1 Best Selling Author of over 80 recipe books.

She is a loving wife and mother who lives on a small farm in Baltimore County, Maryland and has a passion for all things domestic especially when it comes to saving money. She has a profitable eBay business and is a couponing addict. Follow her tips and tricks to learn how to make delicious meals on a budget, save money or to learn the latest life hack!

Visit her Amazon Author Page to see her latest books:

amazon.com/author/laurasommers

Visit the Recipe Lady's blog for even more great recipes and to learn which books are **FREE** for download each week:

http://the-recipe-lady.blogspot.com/

Subscribe to The Recipe Lady blog through Amazon and have recipes and updates sent directly to your Kindle:

The Recipe Lady Blog through Amazon

Laura Sommers is also an Extreme Couponer and Penny Hauler! If you would like to find out how to get things for **FREE** with coupons or how to get things for only a **PENNY**, then visit her couponing blog **Penny Items and Freebies**

http://penny-items-and-freebies.blogspot.com/

© Copyright 2017. Laura Sommers.
All rights reserved.
No part of this book may be reproduced in any form or by any electronic or mechanical means without written permission of the author. All text, illustrations and design are the exclusive property of
Laura Sommers

About the Author ii

Introduction 1

Coffee Pot Ramen Noodles 2

Coffee Pot Peanut Satay..3

Coffee Pot Cheesy Tuna and Noodles 4

Coffee Pot Mac and Cheese 5

Coffee Pot Hot Dogs 6

Coffee Pot Oatmeal 7

Coffee Pot Pesto Chicken 8

Coffee Pot Chocolate Fondue 9

Steamed Coffee Pot Broccoli and Cauliflower 10

Coffee Pot Hot Chocolate 11

Coffee Pot Hard Boiled Eggs 12

Coffee Pot Egg Scramble 13

Coffee pot Egg Salad 14

Coffee Maker Sausage...15

Coffee Pot Rice 16

Coffee Pot Lemon Pepper Chicken 17

Coffee Pot Candied Pecans 18

Hotel Green Beans with Toasted Almonds..19

Coffee Maker Hobo Soup 20

Coffee Maker Grits 21

Coffee Maker Lentils 22

Coffee Maker Spicy Meatballs..23

Coffee Maker Salmon and Veggies 24

Coffee Pot Butter Potatoes	25
Coffee Pot Pesto Potatoes	26
Clothes Iron Quesadilla	27
Clothes Iron Grilled Cheese	28
Clothes Iron Cheese and Ham Panini	29
Clothes Iron Peanut Butter and Jelly	30
Clothes Iron French Toast with Cream Cheese Icing	31
Leftover Chicken Coffee Pot Soup	32
Hotel Pizza English Muffins	33
Hotel Room Tuna Melt	34
Hotel Room Rueben	35
About the Author	36
Other books by Laura Sommers	37

Introduction

Going on vacation can be an exciting and fun experience. But after living for a week or more in a hotel room, your waistline and your wallet will feel the pain. This was true for me after a dream vacation to Disney World.

Eating out can be expensive! And after doing so for a length of time for every meal and you may be begging for something simple or home cooked. This can be true whether your trip is for business or for pleasure. The problem is, many hotels, motels or hostels don't have kitchens so they lack the basic cooking appliances that one needs to cook in their room. Disney World in Orlando is especially guilty of this. But there are other pre-packaged destinations and spas that are guilty of the same. Many places don't even give you a continental breakfast.

So, I looked around the hotel room and figured out that there are three items standard in every hotel room around the world that can be used as make-shift cooking appliances. These are the coffee maker, the clothes iron and the hair dryer. Every hotel also has a mini-fridge so some of the items here will need refrigeration.

Using these appliances and only these appliances, I have created a cookbook full of mouth-watering recipes to satisfy your craving for a home-cooked meal. Every recipe is as simple as possible so the instant variety is used when available.

These recipes are also great for the college student to make in their dorm room. The only thing is that college students usually have a microwave or a toaster to work with but hotel guests often do not.

Take care when making these recipes so that the food, or the room, does not burn. Also, please clean the appliances thoroughly after using them to cook so the next hotel guest does not get butter on their clothes that they try to iron or cinnamon in their coffee that they try to brew.

Enjoy!

Coffee Pot Ramen Noodles

Ingredients:

1 package of Ramen Noodles, any flavor
Water
1 coffee maker

Directions:

1. Crumble the ramen noodles in the package.
2. Add the noodle pieces to the carafe.
3. Add the seasoning.
4. Add about 2 cups of water into the reservoir of the coffee maker.
5. Turn the coffee maker on brew the water.
6. Let the noodles sit in the hot water for however long is specified on the package directions.
7. Pour the noodles and water in a bowl and add your desired toppings.

Coffee Pot Peanut Satay

Ingredients:

8 packets Smucker's peanut butter (or 1/2 cup peanut butter)
1 packet Chinese takeout soy sauce
1/2 packet Chinese takeout spicy mustard
1 tbsp. water
2 tbsps. peanut crumbs
1 packet of crushed red pepper if desired.
1 package of Ramen Noodles, any flavor, spice packet discarded

Directions:

1. Whisk the peanut butter, soy sauce, mustard and water in a bowl until smooth.
2. Add about 2 cups of water into the reservoir of the coffee maker.
3. Turn the coffee maker on brew the water.
4. Let the noodles sit in the hot water for however long is specified on the package directions.
5. Drain the noodles.
6. Add the pasta and coat to toss.
7. Top with the crushed peanuts.
8. Top with the crushed red pepper if desired.
9. Serve and enjoy!

Coffee Pot Cheesy Tuna and Noodles

Ingredients:

1 cup boiling water
1 (3 oz.) package any flavor ramen noodles
1 (3 oz.) can water-packed tuna, drained
2 slices American cheese
1 coffee maker

Directions:

1. Crumble the ramen noodles in the package.
2. Add the noodle pieces to the carafe.
3. Add the seasoning.
4. Add about 2 cups of water into the reservoir of the coffee maker.
5. Turn the coffee maker on brew the water.
6. Let the noodles sit in the hot water for however long is specified on the package directions.
7. Drain and discard water from noodles, then stir in seasoning packet, tuna, and American cheese.
8. Stir until cheese is melted.
9. Serve and enjoy!

Coffee Pot Mac and Cheese

This recipe is for a large carafe coffee maker. If the coffee maker is smaller, adjust as needed.

Ingredients:

8 oz. maccaroni pasta (half a box)
1/2 stick butter
1/2 cup milk
Grated cheddar cheese
Aluminum foil
1 coffee maker
1 tsp. salt

Directions:

1. Put the dried macaroni in the carafe.
2. Add the salt.
3. Pour the maximum amount of water in the reservoir and set to brew.
4. Let cook about 20 minutes, or twice the time on the pasta box directions.
5. Drain the pasta and empty in to a bowl, then set aside.
6. Cut up the butter and put in the carafe.
7. Add the milk.
8. Layer pasta then cheese back in to the carafe until full.
9. Wrap the top of the carafe with aluminum foil.
10. Place the carafe back on the burner and heat until cheese is melted, stirring occasionally, about an hour.
11. Serve and enjoy!

Coffee Pot Hot Dogs

Ingredients:

Water
Hotdogs
Hotdog buns
Ketchup, optional
Mustard, optional
Pickle relish, optional
Raw onions, optional
1 coffee maker

Directions:

1. Place hot dogs in the coffee pot.
2. Run water through the coffeemaker.
3. Let it cook for 15 minutes or until done.
4. Place hotdogs on buns.
5. Add desired toppings such as ketchup, mustard, pickle relish and onions.
6. Serve and enjoy!

Coffee Pot Oatmeal

Ingredients:

2 packets instant oatmeal
Water
1 coffee maker
1 packet jelly or jam, optional
1 packet honey, optional

Directions:

1. Add oatmeal to carafe.
2. Add desired amount of water to carafe.
3. Turn on coffee maker and allow it to heat, about 5 minutes.
4. Add to serving bowls.
5. Add packets of honey or jam if desired.
6. Serve and enjoy!

Coffee Pot Pesto Chicken

Ingredients:

1 pkg. precooked chicken
1 tbsp. pesto
1 tsp. pine nuts
1 pkg. dried spaghetti
Salt to taste

Directions:

1. Add desired amount of spaghetti and water to the carafe.
2. Turn on the coffee maker and cook according to the package directions.
3. You may need to cook pasta a bit longer than recommended.
4. Drain pasta.
5. Add pesto and pine nuts.
6. Salt to taste.
7. Serve and enjoy!

Coffee Pot Chocolate Fondue

Ingredients:

1 cup heavy cream
2 tsp. of vanilla extract
1 cup chocolate chips
Things to Dip:
Pound cake, cut in to squares
Strawberries
Large marshmallows
Pretzel Sticks
Bananas
Pineapple
Apples
Other fruit of choice
1 coffee maker

Directions:

1. Add the cream, vanilla and chocolate to the coffee maker carafe.
2. Turn on the burner and heat until all is melted together.
3. Dip the fruit or pound cake in the chocolate using a fork.
4. Enjoy!

Steamed Coffee Pot Broccoli and Cauliflower

Ingredients:

Broccoli
Cauliflower
Salt and pepper to taste.
Water
1 coffee maker

Directions:

1. Put broccoli and cauliflower in the basket at the top of the coffee maker.
2. Pour the maximum amount of water in the reservoir that the coffee maker takes.
3. "Brew" the water.
4. Pour vegetables in to a bowl and add sault and pepper to taste.
5. Serve and enjoy!

Coffee Pot Hot Chocolate

You can use the coffee pot to boil the water and then just add packets of coco poder, or you can use the ingredients below for a richer more chocately cup.

Ingredients:

1 bag of chocolate chips
Heavy cream
2 cups water
1 coffee maker

Directions:

1. Fill half the carafe with heavy cream then dump in the entire bag of chocolate chips.
2. Brew two cups of water.
3. Let it sit until all the chocolate is melted and blended, stirring occasionally.
4. Serve and enjoy!

Coffee Pot Hard Boiled Eggs

Ingredients:

2 eggs
Salt and pepper
Water
1 coffee maker

Directions:

1. Fill the carafe with water.
2. place the eggs in the carafe.
3. Brew and let sit for 10 to 12 minutes.
4. Douse the eggs in cold water.
5. Peel the eggs.
6. Salt and pepper to taste.
7. Eat and enjoy!

Coffee Pot Egg Scramble

Ingredients:

3 eggs
1 cup grated cheddar cheese
1 cup spinach
1/8 cup milk
Cooking spray
1 coffee maker
Salt and pepper to taste

Directions:

1. Spray the inside bottom of the coffee pot with cooking spray.
2. Heat the coffee maker.
3. Whisk the eggs and milk in a separate bowl.
4. Add cheese to the eggs and milk.
5. Pour the egg mixture into the coffee pot.
6. Add spinach.
7. Heat for six minutes, or until the eggs are cooked.
8. Ad salt and pepper.
9. Serve and enjoy!

Coffee pot Egg Salad

Ingredients:

3 eggs
Salt and pepper
3 mayonnaise packets
1 mustard packet
2 slices of bread
Water
1 coffee maker

Directions:

1. Fill the carafe with water.
2. place the eggs in the carafe.
3. Brew and let sit for 10 to 12 minutes.
4. Douse the eggs in cold water.
5. Peel the eggs.
6. Add eggs to bowl and chop them up with a fork.
7. Add mayonnaise, mustard and salt and pepper.
8. Spread between two pieces of bread to make a sandwich.
9. Eat and enjoy!

Coffee Maker Sausage

Ingredients:

Brown and serve sausage links.
1 coffee maker
Cooking spray

Directions:

1. Remove the carafe from the heating service.
2. Turn on the coffee maker to heat the burner, but don't start any brewing.
3. Spray with cooking spray.
4. Heat the sausage on the burner until browned.
5. Serve and enjoy!

Coffee Pot Rice

Ingredients:

1 pkg. instant rice
Water
1 coffee maker

Directions:

1. Add rice to carafe.
2. Add water specified by the package directions to reservoir.
3. Turn on the coffee maker and set it to brew for about 10 minutes.
4. Serve and enjoy!

Coffee Pot Lemon Pepper Chicken

Ingredients:

1 chicken breast
Lemon pepper seasoning
Water
1 coffee maker

Directions:

1. Add chicken to the coffee pot.
2. Add enough water to cover about a quarter of it.
3. Add lemon pepper seasoning.
4. Turn on the coffee maker, and cook for about 15 minutes on each side.
5. Check that the chicken is no longer pink inside.
6. Serve and enjoy!

Coffee Pot Candied Pecans

Ingredients:

1 cup pecans, shelled
2 tbsps. sugar
2 pinches salt
1 pinch chili flakes, optional
1 cup water

Directions:

1. Put sugar and salt in coffee pot.
2. Add chili flakes if desired.
3. Run water through the brewer.
4. Mix to combine.
5. Add the pecans.
6. Let the pecans sit for five minutes in the coffee pot.
7. Let stand before drying the nuts—this recipe even suggests using a blowdryer to speed up the process.
8. Finally, use the coffee maker's burner to toast the pecans, turning occasionally.

Hotel Green Beans with Toasted Almonds

Ingredients:

1/2 pound green beans
1 tbsp. butter
1 lemon
1/8 cup almonds
1 coffee maker
Paper towel
Aluminum foil
1 Iron/Ironing board

Directions:

1. Wash and trim green beans in sink.
2. Place beans in coffee maker basket.
3. Run coffee maker cycle 3-4 times, or until desired tenderness is reached.
4. Drain beans on a paper towel.
5. Meanwhile, place almonds between two sheets of aluminum foil in a single layer.
6. Press iron onto aluminum foil and hold for 10 seconds. Repeat until the entire surface of the foil has been covered.
7. While coffee warmer is still hot, place butter in empty coffee carafe and return to warmer to melt butter. Squeeze the juice of the lemon into the butter. Swirl to mix.
8. Return beans to carafe and toss to coat.
9. Serve beans topped with toasted almonds.

Coffee Maker Hobo Soup

This is tomato soup made from the free ketchup and other packets that are available in the break room of the hotel or any other place that they sell food.
If you are tired of spending tons of money on food eating out during your business trip or vacation. Or if you just need a quick snack, try this tomato soup made only from condiment packets.

Ingredients:

8 packets of ketchup
2 packets of sugar
1 cup water
2 packets salt, or to taste
2 packets pepper, or to taste
2 packets saltine crackers
Water

Directions:

1. Add ketchup, sugar and water to carafe.
2. Stir to mix.
3. Turn on the burner and heat the soup.
4. Let simmer 10-15 minutes, until heated through, stirring occationally until blended.
5. Add salt and pepper to taste.
6. Serve with saltine crackers and enjoy!
7. Note: Add two mini cups of non-dairy creamer to make creamy tomato hobo soup.

Coffee Maker Grits

Ingredients:

2 cups water
1 1/4 cups milk
1 tsp. salt
1 cup quick cooking grits
1/2 cup butter

Directions:

1. Put the water, milk and salt in the coffee pot.
2. Turn on the coffee maker and heat the water until hot.
3. Add grits a little bit at a time.
4. Stir until grits are well mixed.
5. Put the carafe back on the burner and cook for 30 minutes, stirring occasionally.
6. Add more water if necessary.
7. Grits are done when they have the consistency of smooth cream of wheat.
8. Stir in half the butter with the pot of grits until melted.
9. Add grits to serving bowls and divide the remaining butter among the portions by putting on top of each portion.

Coffee Maker Lentils

Ingredients:

1/2 cup dried lentils
1 cup of water (or enough to cover the lentils)
1 carrot, peeled and cut in to pieces
1 stalk celery, cut in to pieces
1 sm. onion, peeled, cut in to pieces
1 bay leaf
Salt and pepper to taste.

Directions:

1. Add all ingredients to the coffee pot, except the salt.
2. Add enough water to cover the ingredients.
3. Turn on the coffee maker and let it brew or simmer for 1/2 hour, or until the lentils are tender.
4. Add salt and pepper to taste.
5. Serve and enjoy!

Coffee Maker Spicy Meatballs

Ingredients:

Meatballs
1 tbsp. sesame seeds
4 oz. Of our favorite Hot Sauce

Directions:

1. Put the Meatballs into a bowl with hot water to pre-heat them
2. Insulate the pot by wrapping the coffee pot with a layer of tinfoil
3. Place pre-heated meatballs in the coffee pot, do not include the water
4. Put back on the burner
5. Run water through the coffeemaker
6. Cover the top with a double layer of foil and cook for 40 minutes
7. Drain water from the pot
8. Add 4 oz. hot sauce and sesame seeds
9. Cover and put back on the burner for another 20 minutes to heat the sauce

Coffee Maker Salmon and Veggies

Ingredients:

Salmon
1 handful broccoli
1 handful cauliflower
2 tbsp. soy sauce
1 tbsp. brown sugar
1 tsp. salt
1/2 tsp. crushed garlic
Lemon

Directions:

1. Blanch veggies by putting them where the coffee grounds go
2. Allow hot water to run through the veggies
3. Put the soy sauce, brown sugar, salt and garlic in the coffee pot
4. Place the salmon skin side up in the marinade of the coffee pot
5. Fill pot with enough water to fully submerge the fish
6. Once the fish is submerged leave it for 20 minutes

Coffee Pot Butter Potatoes

Ingredients:

2 cups instant mashed potatoes
1 3/4 cups water
1/4 cup milk
Butter to taste
1 tbsp. butter
1/2 tsp. salt or to taste
Pepper to taste

Directions:

1. Add instant potatoes to the coffee pot.
2. Check the package directions for the correct amount of liquid for the potatoes and adjust milk and water accordingly.
3. Add milk and water then stir to combine.
4. Heat coffee maker and allow potatoes to cook until heated through.
5. Add pesto and olive oil and stir.
6. Add salt and cheese.
7. Stir to combine.
8. Serve and enjoy!

Coffee Pot Pesto Potatoes

Ingredients:

2 cups instant mashed potatoes
1 3/4 cups water
1/4 cup milk
Butter to taste
1 tbsp. pesto
1 tbsp. olive oil
1/2 tsp. salt or to taste
Parmesan cheese

Directions:

1. Add instant potatoes to the coffee pot.
2. Check the package directions for the correct amount of liquid for the potatoes and adjust milk and water accordingly.
3. Add milk and water then stir to combine.
4. Heat coffee maker and allow potatoes to cook until heated through.
5. Add pesto and olive oil and stir.
6. Add salt and cheese.
7. Stir to combine.
8. Serve and enjoy!

Clothes Iron Quesadilla

Ingredients:

1 tortilla
Cheese
Other ingredients such as onion, peppers, etc.
Aluminum foil
1 clothes iron

Directions:

1. Add cheese and other ingredients to the tortilla.
2. Fold the tortilla in half.
3. Fold the foil around the tortilla.
4. Heat each side for about two minutes each.
5. The tortilla should be a nice golden brown.
6. Serve and enjoy.

Clothes Iron Grilled Cheese

Ingredients:

2 slices of bread (hard crusted is best).
Butter
1 slice of cheese
2 slices of tomato, optional
2 slices of onion, optional
Black pepper, optional
Aluminum foil
1 clothes iron

Directions:

1. Turn the iron on and let it heat up (cotton setting).
2. Place a square of aluminum foil large enough to wrap the sandwich on your work area.
3. Butter one side of one slice of bread and place it (butter side down) on the foil.
4. Put the cheese and optional ingredients (tomato, onion, pepper) on one slice of bread.
5. Butter one side of the other slice of bread and place it on top of the other half of the sandwich, butter side up.
6. Wrap the sandwich in the foil.
7. Place the hot iron on top of your sandwich and let it cook for 4 minutes.
8. Flip the sandwich over and place the iron on the other side for 4 minutes.
9. Serve and enjoy!

Clothes Iron Cheese and Ham Panini

Ingredients:

Bread
1 slice of cheese
2 slices of ham
Butter

Directions:

1. Turn the iron on and let it heat up (cotton setting).
2. Place a square of aluminum foil large enough to wrap the sandwich on your work area.
3. Butter one side of one slice of bread and place it (butter side down) on the foil.
4. Put the cheese and ham on one slice of bread.
5. Butter one side of the other slice of bread and place it on top of the other half of the sandwich, butter side up.
6. Wrap the sandwich in the foil.
7. Place the hot iron on top of your sandwich and let it cook for 4 minutes.
8. Flip the sandwich over and place the iron on the other side for 4 minutes.
9. Serve and enjoy!
10. Note: Paninis and grilled sandwiches can also be done on the burner for the coffee pot.

Clothes Iron Peanut Butter and Jelly

Ingredients:

2 slices of bread (hard crusted is best).
Butter
Peanut Butter
Jelly or jam of choice (whatever is available from the hotel break room)
Aluminum foil
1 clothes iron

Directions:

1. Turn the iron on and let it heat up (cotton setting).
2. Place a square of aluminum foil large enough to wrap the sandwich on your work area.
3. Butter one side of one slice of bread and place it (butter side down) on the foil.
4. Spread the peanut butter and jelly on the other side of the slice of bread.
5. Butter one side of the other slice of bread and place it on top of the other half of the sandwich, butter side up.
6. Wrap the sandwich in the foil.
7. Place the hot iron on top of your sandwich and let it cook for 4 minutes.
8. Flip the sandwich over and place the iron on the other side for 4 minutes.
9. Serve and enjoy!

Clothes Iron French Toast with Cream Cheese Icing

Get the packets from the hotel break room or the rest stop on the road.

Ingredients:

4 Philadelphia cream cheese packets
4 tabs of butter (or one tbsp.)
6 packets of sugar
2 eggs
7 mini cups non-dairy creamer
1 tsp. cinnamon
2 Slices of bread
1 clothes iron
Cooking spray

Directions:

1. Cover the bottom of the clothes iron with aluminum foil.
2. Place the iron, bottom up, between two roled towels.
3. Spray the bottom of the foil covered iron with cooking spray.
4. Heat the iron to cotton setting.
5. Mix the eggs, six non-dairy creamer cups, two packets of sugar and cinnamon in a bowl.
6. Lay down a sheet of aluminum foil on the ironing board.
7. Dip the bread in the egg mixture then gently place it on the iron.
8. Cook for 3-5 minutes and then gently turn it over using your fork, or spatula if you have one.
9. Cook for another 3-5 minutes on the other side or until golden brown.
10. Using a fork in a bowl, mix the cream cheese, butter, one non-dairy creamer cup and four packets of sugar.
11. Drizzle over the French toast.
12. Serve and enjoy!

Leftover Chicken Coffee Pot Soup

Ingredients:

6 sprigs thyme
2 bay leaves
2 strips lemon zest (1-inch thick)
2 cloves garlic (crushed)
1 piece fresh ginger (1-inch, sliced)
6 whole black peppercorns
4 cups variety frozen vegetables, such as peas, carrots and corn
2 cups leftover chicken, shredded
1 tbsp. kosher salt
1/4 tsp. ground cumin
1/2 tsp. ground coriander
1/2 tsp. onion powder
1/2 tsp. garlic powder
1 pinch cayenne
1/2 tsp. curry powder
2 tbsps. butter
2 tbsps. chopped cilantro
2 tbsps. chopped basil

Directions:

1. Place a filter in a coffee maker.
2. In the filter, add the thyme, bay leaves, lemon zest, garlic, ginger, and peppercorns. Close the filter.
3. Fill the coffee maker with 6 cups of water.
4. In the carafe, add the vegetables and chicken.
5. Add the salt, coriander, cumin, onion powder, garlic powder, cayenne, curry powder and butter.
6. Turn the coffee maker on to brew, allowing the filtered broth to drip into the carafe and warm the vegetables and chicken. Garnish with cilantro and basil. Serve into mugs and enjoy!
7. Serve and enjoy!

Hotel Pizza English Muffins

Ingredients:

1 English muffin, split, or bagel
4 tbsp. pizza sauce
Mozzarella cheese
Italian seasoning
Parmesan Cheese
Pepperoni slices
1 clothes iron
1 hair dryer
1 coffee maker

Directions:

1. Heat the iron to cotton setting.
2. Place a sheet of aluminum foil on the ironing board.
3. Place the split English muffin on the foil.
4. lay the iron on top of the English muffin halves. You can probably lay the iron on both at once.
5. Iron the muffin halves for 5-10 minutes, or until toasted.
6. Put pizza sauce in the coffee pot carafe.
7. Turn on the coffee maker for 5-10 minutes to heat up the sauce.
8. Stir occasionally until the sauce is heated.
9. Spread sauce on the English muffin halves.
10. Sprinkle with Italian seasoning.
11. Add mozzarella cheese.
12. Add a few slices of pepperoni.
13. Take the hotel blow dryer and use it to heat the cheese until it melts.
14. Sprinkle with grated Parmesian cheese.
15. Serve and enjoy!

Hotel Room Tuna Melt

Ingredients:

1 English muffin or bagel, split
1 pouch of tuna fish
2 packets of mayonnaise
2 packets of pickle relish
2 slices of American cheese
Salt and pepper to taste
Aluminum foil
1 clothes iron
1 hair dryer

Directions:

1. Heat the iron to cotton setting.
2. Lay a sheet of aluminum foil down on the ironing board.
3. Place the English muffin down on the foil.
4. Lay the iron on top of the English muffin halves and leave for 5-10 minutes or until toasted.
5. In a bowl, mix together the tuna, mayonnaise, pickle relish and salt and pepper.
6. Spoon the tuna mixture on to the English muffin halves.
7. Lay slices of cheese on top.
8. Use the hair dryer to melt the cheese.
9. Serve and enjoy!

Hotel Room Rueben

Ingredients:

2 slices rye bread
2 slices of corned beef
1 can sauerkraut
4 packets mayonnaise
1 packet ketchup
2 packets pickle relish
2 slices of Swiss cheese
Salt and pepper to taste
Aluminum foil
1 coffee maker
1 clothes iron
1 hair dryer

Directions:

1. Heat the iron to cotton setting.
2. Lay a sheet of aluminum foil down on the ironing board.
3. Place the rye bread down on the foil side by side.
4. Lay the iron on top of the breadand leave for 5-10 minutes or until toasted.
5. In a bowl, mix together mayonnaise, ketchup, relish and salt and pepper to make the thousand island dressing.
6. Spread the dressing on the rye bread pieces.
7. Lay slices of corned beef on top.
8. Open the can of sauerkraut and pour it in to the coffee pot.
9. Turn on the coffee pot burner to heat the sauerkraut.
10. Strain some the kraut and lay it on the corned beef.
11. Lay slices of Swiss cheese on top of the kraut.
12. Use the hair dryer on high setting to melt the cheese.
13. Serve and enjoy!

About the Author

Laura Sommers is **The Recipe Lady!**

She is the #1 Best Selling Author of over 80 recipe books.

She is a loving wife and mother who lives on a small farm in Baltimore County, Maryland and has a passion for all things domestic especially when it comes to saving money. She has a profitable eBay business and is a couponing addict. Follow her tips and tricks to learn how to make delicious meals on a budget, save money or to learn the latest life hack!

Visit her Amazon Author Page to see her latest books:

amazon.com/author/laurasommers

Visit the Recipe Lady's blog for even more great recipes and to learn which books are **FREE** for download each week:

http://the-recipe-lady.blogspot.com/

Subscribe to The Recipe Lady blog through Amazon and have recipes and updates sent directly to your Kindle:

The Recipe Lady Blog through Amazon

Laura Sommers is also an Extreme Couponer and Penny Hauler! If you would like to find out how to get things for **FREE** with coupons or how to get things for only a **PENNY**, then visit her couponing blog **Penny Items and Freebies**

http://penny-items-and-freebies.blogspot.com/

Other books by Laura Sommers

- Easy to Make Party Dip Recipes: Chips and Dips and Salsa and Whips!
- Super Slimming Vegan Soup Recipes!
- Popcorn Lovers Recipe Book
- Inexpensive Low Carb Recipes
- Recipes for the Zombie Apocalypse: Cooking Meals with Shelf Stable Foods
- Best Traditional Irish Recipes for St. Patrick's Day
- Awesome Sugar Free Diabetic Pie Recipes

May all of your meals be a banquet
with good friends and good food.

Printed in Great Britain
by Amazon